How Astronauts Use Math

by Mary Hense

**Math Curriculum Consultant: Rhea A. Stewart, M.A.,
Specialist in Mathematics, Science,
and Technology Education**

An Imprint of Chelsea House Publishers

Math in the Real World: How Astronauts Use Math

Copyright © 2010 by Infobase Publishing

Chelsea Clubhouse
An imprint of Chelsea House Publishers
132 West 31st Street
New York NY 10001

Library of Congress Cataloging-in-Publication Data
Hense, Mary.
        How astronauts use math / by Mary Hense.
            p. cm. — (Math in the real world)
        Includes bibliographical references and index.
        ISBN 978-1-60413-610-4
        1. Astronautics—Mathematics—Juvenile literature. 2. Astronauts—Juvenile literature. I. Title.
    TL849.H46 2010
    510.24'6294--dc22   2009023926

Chelsea Clubhouse books are available at special discounts when purchased in bulk quantities for businesses, associations, institutions, or sales promotions. Please call our Special Sales Department in New York at (212) 967-8800 or (800) 322-8755.

You can find Chelsea Clubhouse on the World Wide Web at http://www.chelseahouse.com

Developed for Chelsea House by RJF Publishing LLC (www.RJFpublishing.com)
Text and cover design by Tammy West/Westgraphix LLC
Illustrations by Spectrum Creative Inc.
Photo research by Edward A. Thomas
Index by Nila Glikin

Photo Credits: 4, 5, 6, 12, 14, 15, 18, 21, 22, 23, 24, 25: NASA; 10: NASA, ESA, P. Challis and R. Kirshner (Harvard-Smithsonian Center for Astrophysics); 16: BioServe Space Technologies at the University of Colorado; 26: NASA/Regina Mitchell-Ryall.

Printed and bound in the United States of America

Bang RJF 10 9 8 7 6 5 4 3 2 1

This book is printed on acid-free paper.

All links and Web addresses were checked and verified to be correct at the time of publication. Because of the dynamic nature of the Web, some addresses and links may have changed since publication and may no longer be valid.

Table of Contents

Answers and helpful hints for the You Do the Math
activities are in the Answer Key.

Words that are defined in the Glossary are
in **bold** type the first time they appear in the text.

Countdown

A t 3 hours before liftoff, or *T minus 3 hours*, 7 astronauts finish dressing in orange **NASA** spacesuits at the Kennedy Space Center in Florida. They step into a bus that takes them to the shuttle launch pad. As they exit the bus, the astronauts seem small compared to the 122-foot-tall **orbiter** that will be their home for the next two weeks.

A shuttle crew heads for the launch pad for a 2007 flight.

The Last Few Hours

T minus 2 hours 30 minutes: The astronauts travel by elevator to a walkway. They put on parachutes, boots, and caps. One by one, the astronauts enter the space-craft. Once seated, they put on their helmets and buckle up.

T minus 20 minutes and holding: The countdown clock stops for about 10 minutes. The astronauts and people at Mission Control talk on a radio. They review their plans.

T minus 7 minutes 30 seconds: The walkway pulls away from the shuttle door.

T minus 2 minutes: The astronauts lower the **visors** on their helmets to cover their faces.

T minus 6.60 seconds: The orbiter's main engine 3 starts.

T minus 6.48 seconds: Main engine 2 starts.

T minus 6.36 seconds: Main engine 1 starts.

T minus 0 minutes: Eight bolts that hold the **solid rocket boosters** to the launch pad explode. The solid rocket boosters ignite. Liftoff!

The shuttle Endeavour on the launch pad shortly before liftoff.

You Do the Math

Countdown Schedule

Astronauts use schedules from planning to landing. A countdown is a type of schedule. Look at the countdown on pages 4 and 5. How many minutes and seconds do the astronauts have from the time the walkway starts to move to the time they lower their visors?

Liftoff

A t liftoff, the space shuttle seems to climb as fast as a crowded elevator car. Below the astronauts, fuel burns at a temperature of 6,000 degrees Fahrenheit (°F). That is 3,500°F more than it takes to melt steel!

The Space Shuttle System

The parts of the space shuttle system work together. The **external tank** fuels the orbiter's three main engines with 6 parts liquid oxygen to 1 part liquid hydrogen. The two solid rocket boosters, called *solid* because of their solid fuel mixture, provide more than $\frac{3}{4}$ of the **thrust** during liftoff and the first stage of the flight. Thrust is the force that moves the shuttle.

The solid rocket boosters give the astronauts a bumpy ride for 2 minutes. That is the time it takes to go 28 miles.

Flight directors on the ground track the progress of shuttle missions and communicate with the astronauts.

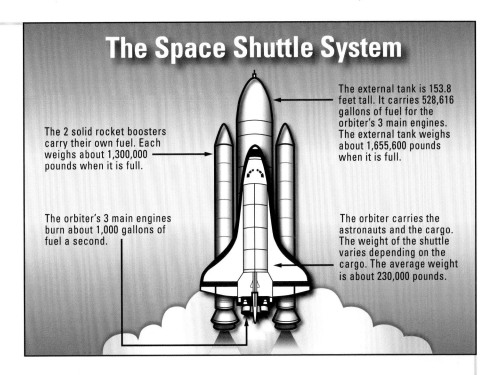

The Space Shuttle System

The external tank is 153.8 feet tall. It carries 528,616 gallons of fuel for the orbiter's 3 main engines. The external tank weighs about 1,655,600 pounds when it is full.

The 2 solid rocket boosters carry their own fuel. Each weighs about 1,300,000 pounds when it is full.

The orbiter's 3 main engines burn about 1,000 gallons of fuel a second.

The orbiter carries the astronauts and the cargo. The weight of the shuttle varies depending on the cargo. The average weight is about 230,000 pounds.

By then, the solid rocket boosters are low on fuel. The astronauts hear a pop when the bolts that secure the boosters to the external tank explode. The freed solid rocket boosters fly in an arc. Then, they parachute to the ocean.

The ride is smoother without the solid rocket boosters. The three main engines accelerate the orbiter from about 3,000 miles per hour to about 17,000 miles per hour, making the astronauts feel 3 times as heavy as they do on Earth.

You Do the Math

The Space Shuttle's Weight

The three main engines and two solid rocket boosters produce a total of 7.8 million pounds of thrust. For the space shuttle to move upward, it has to weigh less than 7.8 million pounds. Use the diagram above. About how much does the space shuttle system weigh? Hint: Round each number to the greatest place value.

In Earth Orbit

About 8.5 minutes after liftoff, the external tank is almost empty. The astronauts turn off the orbiter's main engines. The external tank ejects, and it burns up in the atmosphere. The external tank is the only part of the space shuttle system that isn't reusable. For the astronauts in the orbiter, the ride is now quiet and smooth—even at a speed of 17,000 miles per hour!

Turning the Orbiter

In space, the shuttle **orbits** (moves in a path around) Earth. While it's

Astronauts fire small rockets called thrusters to rotate the shuttle. Astronauts fire opposite thrusters to stop the rotation.

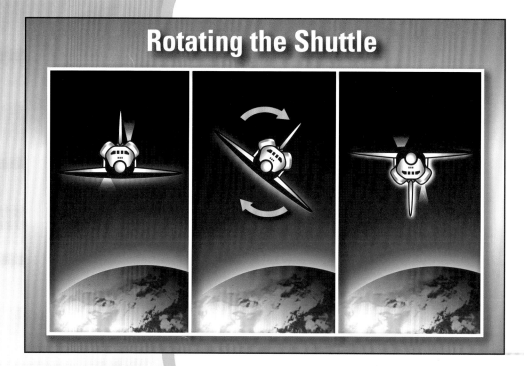

Rotating the Shuttle

in orbit, the nose of the orbiter can point in any direction. The pilot can rotate (turn) the orbiter by firing **thrusters**, or small rocket engines.

Sometimes the pilot positions the orbiter to face backward and upside down. When the orbiter is in this position, the three main engines face into the direction of the orbit. The engines shield the orbiter from debris in the orbiter's path. The crew won't use the main engines again, so any damage to the engines won't affect the crew's safety. The sturdy belly of the orbiter faces away from Earth. Tiles on the belly protect the orbiter from meteorites coming from space and from the heat of the Sun. The window side of the orbiter faces Earth. The windows give the astronauts a good view of Earth.

You Do the Math

Temperature Extremes

Objects in space must be able to withstand, or survive, extreme temperature ranges. The side of the orbiter that faces away from Earth can get as hot as 250°F. The side that faces Earth can get as cold as ‑150°F. What is the temperature range? Hint: Using a thermometer or a number line (see below) may be helpful. Start at ‑150, and count by 50s to 250.

‑150 ‑100 ‑50 0 50 100 150 200 250

Rendezvous in Space

Objects that orbit are **satellites**. A shuttle orbiter, the International Space Station, the Hubble Space Telescope, and the Moon are satellites. The International Space Station is the largest artificial satellite in space. Astronauts use the station as a base for research and exploration. The Hubble Space Telescope is an **observatory** in space.

Orbits may differ in altitude. A shuttle orbiter can orbit as high as 400 miles above Earth. Compare that altitude to others shown in the table on page 11. Though 400 miles is far from the altitudes of stationary weather satellites and the Moon, the International Space Station and the Hubble telescope are within an orbiter's reach.

A shuttle mission may bring a new crew to the space station. Shuttle astronauts may need to replace parts on the Hubble telescope or make other repairs to it.

There are no clouds, smog, or city lights 360 miles above Earth, so the Hubble telescope gets clear views of distant stars, as in the image above. The "ring of pearls" surrounds an exploding star.

Orbit Altitudes	
Satellite	Approximate Altitude (in miles)
International Space Station	220
Hubble Space Telescope	360
Stationary Weather Satellites	22,300
Moon	240,000

Orbits and Speeds

Earth's mass affects orbiting objects. The lower the orbit, the faster the orbiting object's speed. The higher the orbit, the slower the object's speed. For example, the lower International Space Station orbits Earth at a speed of about 17,500 miles per hour. A higher stationary weather satellite orbits Earth at a speed of about 7,000 miles per hour. The speed of a stationary weather satellite is the same as the speed of Earth's rotation on its axis. The weather satellite orbits in the same direction as Earth's rotation, so it appears to stay in one location, or be stationary, over Earth.

Suppose astronauts on the space shuttle are in the same orbit as the Hubble telescope but are lagging behind. To catch up, astronauts drop to a lower orbit. They go faster in the lower orbit. Then, when they catch up, they fire thrusters to lift the space shuttle into Hubble's orbit again.

You Do the Math

Computing Distances in Space

Use the table above. What is the difference in miles between the altitudes of the Hubble telescope and the International Space Station?

Microgravity

A stronauts on the shuttle weigh a little less than they do on Earth. This is because the pull of Earth's gravity is less a few hundred miles above Earth than it is on the ground. Gravity is a force that pulls objects toward each other. Weight is a measure of the strength of the pull of Earth's gravity on a person or a thing. When the pull of gravity on an astronaut decreases, so does the astronaut's weight.

Freefalling

Many people have seen photos of astronauts floating within an orbiting spacecraft. The astronauts may seem

Shuttle astronauts reach for some fresh fruit floating by in the microgravity of the orbiter.

to have no weight. This is not true, though. Astronauts weigh a little less, but they still have weight.

Astronauts feel weightless and float because they are free-falling. People on a theme park roller coaster experience free-falling. When the roller coaster car plummets (drops), they might feel as if they're floating in air.

Think of throwing a ball. The ball arches skyward and then downward in a freefall. An ant riding on the ball would feel weightless on the way down. Suppose you threw the ball at a speed of 17,500 miles an hour in a curve at least 150 miles high. The ball and the ant would go into orbit, and the ant would feel weightless. The ball and the ant would be freefalling around Earth. Shuttle astronauts are constantly falling in a curve that continues around Earth as an orbit. Astronauts floating in a spacecraft and feeling weightless are experiencing a condition called **microgravity.**

You Do the Math

Weight and Height

In space, without the same weight on an astronuat's spine, or back-bone, an astronaut might be $\frac{3}{4}$ inch taller than on Earth. Suppose an astronaut is 5 feet $9\frac{1}{2}$ inches tall on Earth. How tall might that astronaut be in space?

The International Space Station

How do you get a space station that weighs 940,000 pounds and is 356 feet wide and 290 feet long into space?

Russian scientists solved that problem. When they were constructing the older Mir space station, they built and moved one section, or module, of the space station at a time. People from 16 countries built the larger International Space Station in the same way.

Each module is like a room of a house. On Earth, scientists and engineers made precise measurements, so that the modules would fit together in space without any leaks.

The Leonardo canister is shown here in the payload bay of a shuttle orbiter.

Sometimes, space-craft with no people onboard carried modules to the International Space Station. Sometimes, astronauts and **cosmonauts** (Russian astronauts) took modules and supplies to the space station.

This picture shows the International Space Station as seen from the shuttle orbiter Discovery during a 2009 mission.

Carrying Cargo in Leonardo

Some supplies travel to the space station in a **canister** named Leonardo. Leonardo takes its name from the Italian painter and inventor Leonardo da Vinci. The Italian Space Agency built Leonardo to fit snuggly in the space shuttle orbiter's **payload bay**. This is the section of the orbiter for storing cargo.

The Leonardo canister is shaped like a cylinder. It is 15 feet in diameter and 21 feet long. Its volume is about 3,709 cubic feet.

You Do the Math

Filling and Emptying Leonardo

The Leonardo canister weighs 4.5 tons when it is empty. On one space shuttle mission, Leonardo carried about 32,000 pounds of supplies to the space station. How many tons did Leonardo weigh before astronauts emptied it? (Hint: 1 ton equals 2,000 pounds.)

Working in Space

Astronauts spend most of their time in space working. They repair equipment on the International Space Station, on the Hubble telescope, or on other satellites orbiting Earth. Sometimes, they install new equipment. They study Earth and space, and they study their own health in space. Sometimes, they perform experiments.

Spiders in Space

In one experiment, students and astronauts wanted to find out how spiders would spin webs in microgravity. In their classrooms on Earth, students watched spiders make webs. At the same time, astronauts watched space

Spiders in space first made a web that looked like tangled threads (below). Their second attempt (below, right) was much more like webs made on Earth.

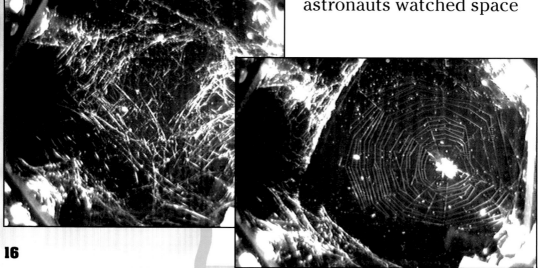

spiders they had taken up with them make webs. Students and astronauts shared their observations and compared pictures of the webs.

The space spiders' first attempt at making a web looked like tangled threads. The spiders took down the web and tried again. The second time, they were more successful. The second space web was flat, and it had more symmetry. The second space web contained **polygons**, as spider webs on Earth do. It seemed that the spiders were able to adjust to the microgravity environment.

You Do the Math

Numbering Missions

The Space Transportation System (STS) is the name for the shuttle program. Each shuttle mission has an STS number. During the planning stages, people at NASA number missions in order. The first mission was STS-1 in 1981. The table below shows the numbers of some missions. Write the mission numbers in order from least to greatest.

Some Space Shuttle Missions	
Orbiter	**Mission**
Atlantis	STS-43
Atlantis	STS-115
Discovery	STS-120
Discovery	STS-105
Endeavour	STS-126
Endeavour	STS-113

Spacewalk

Astronauts sometimes work outside the shuttle orbiter or the space station. To do so, they wear a spacesuit. A spacesuit has 14 layers. The layers protect astronauts from such things as extreme temperatures, tiny meteorites, and the lack of air pressure.

The inside of a spacesuit can get warm from an astronaut's body heat, especially if the astronaut moves around a lot. Cool water runs through 300 feet of tubes near the astronaut's skin to keep the astronaut comfortable.

The astronaut wears what looks like a backpack. Inside are oxygen tanks for breathing, a small thruster for moving, and a radio system for talking to other crew members.

Practice, Practice, Practice

It takes practice to feel comfortable in a spacesuit. Tools can feel awkward in padded hands. Unless astronauts brace themselves, objects

An astronaut at work during a spacewalk at the International Space Station.

that astronauts try to move might move the astronauts instead!

For each hour of a spacewalk, an astronaut practices for 7 hours on Earth. So an astronaut planning to spacewalk for 6 hours practices for 42 hours ($6 \times 7 = 42$).

How long does a spacewalk usually last? To figure that out, you can use **data**. By the end of 2008, astronauts had logged about 749 total hours in 119 different spacewalks at the International Space Station. So, if you divide the number of hours by the number of spacewalks, that makes the **average** length of a spacewalk more than 6 hours ($749 \div 119 \approx 6.3$ hours; the meaning of the symbol $\approx$ is "approximately equal to").

You Do the Math

Carrying the Weight

Moving objects in microgravity is easier than moving those same objects on Earth. It isn't that easy, though. The objects still have mass. (Mass is the amount of matter in an object.) It takes energy to move mass. The table below shows some objects an astronaut might be carrying around at one time. What is the total weight of those objects on Earth?

Objects Carried	
Object	**Weight on Earth (in pounds)**
Spacesuit	315
Toolbox	34
Telescope Sensor	437

Foods for Space

Astronauts need good nutrition and balanced meals in space. At the Space Food Systems Laboratory in Houston, Texas, experts invent recipes and packaging for healthful space food. They also make sure the food is tasty by having astronauts taste and rate the items that they cook up.

The astronauts give each food item they sample ratings from 1 to 9, where 1 is the worst rating, and 9 is the best. Foods with an average score of 6 or better have a good chance of accompanying the astronauts on their mission. Ratings for a beef stew are shown below. Does this stew pass the test?

Beef Stew	
Rate from 1 to 9	
1 for worst, 9 for best	
appearance	5
color	7
smell	9
taste	8
texture	6
Total points:	35
Score (average):	7

The beef stew passed the test with an average score of 7. To calculate the average, add the points, then divide the sum by the number of addends:

$$5 + 7 + 9 + 8 + 6 = 35$$
$$35 \div 5 = 7$$

An American astronaut (left) and a Russian cosmonaut share a meal aboard the International Space Station.

Cooking and Drinking in Space

Astronauts eat some fresh foods in space, such as fruits and vegetables. They also eat foods that are prepared ahead of time on Earth. These foods may be freeze-dried. (They are frozen, and then water in the foods is removed.)

In space, astronauts have kitchens, called **galleys**. Galleys have ovens to warm food. It takes 20 to 30 minutes to heat food to about 170°F.

Spilled milk is nothing to cry about. It is a geometric treat. If a liquid is released in space, it forms a floating sphere. An astronaut can poke a straw into it and drink the liquid.

You Do the Math

Enough Food for the Mission

Each astronaut eats about 3 pounds of food a day. Not counting extra emergency supplies, about how many pounds of food would 5 astronauts need for a 14-day mission?

Exercise and Recreation

To keep bones and muscles strong during space missions, astronauts use exercise machines. Exercise is a daily event on astronauts' schedules. Astronauts often exercise for more than 2 hours each day, 7 days a week, or about 14 hours a week.

Astronauts use three main types of exercise equipment. They pedal on a stationary bicycle. They walk or jog on a treadmill. They work out with a machine that is similar to a weight-lifting machine.

Free Time

For shuttle astronauts, free time is rare because the astronauts usually have only a week or two to complete mission objectives. Crew members on the space station stay for months. Though they work during most waking hours Monday through Friday, they have free time in the mornings and evenings. When they wake up, they have about $1\frac{1}{2}$ hours to shower,

Astronaut Greg Chamitoff plays chess with an opponent on Earth while aboard the International Space Station.

eat breakfast, and get ready for work. Right before bedtime, astronauts have about 2 hours to e-mail friends and relatives and to relax.

Friday night is movie night, and sometimes Saturday night, too. During the weekends, the space station astronauts enjoy more time off. On Saturday they might volunteer to do science for a few hours or finish up a project that is behind schedule. On Sunday astronauts see and talk to their families by video conferencing. The rest of the weekend astronauts might take pictures, read, listen to music, play musical instruments, play games, and enjoy the views of Earth and space.

Astronaut Ellen Ochoa played her flute when she was on the space station. Astronaut Greg Chamitoff used his spare time to challenge students at Stevenson Elementary School in Bellevue, Washington, to the Earth vs. Space Chess Match.

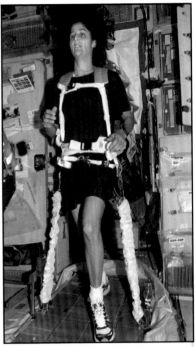

Astronaut Sunita Williams uses a treadmill on the International Space Station during a 2007 mission.

You Do the Math

Miles on the Bike

To study the effect of exercise on people in a microgravity environment, astronauts sometimes keep exercise records. Suppose an astronaut recorded these daily bicycle machine distances in miles: 5.6, 4.3, 3.7, 4.8, 6.4, 5.0, 5.2. What is the average number of miles that the astronaut pedaled each day?

Sleep

A stronauts need to get 8 hours of sleep in every 24-hour period in order to keep alert and to think clearly. Getting that much sleep is not always easy. One reason is that the shuttle is orbiting Earth so quickly that the periods of light and darkness are much shorter than on Earth. With the Sun rising every 90 minutes, it can be hard for an astronaut to know when it's bedtime.

Astronauts rely on clocks and schedules to know when to sleep. Mission Control on Earth wakes shuttle astronauts by playing popular songs. On the International Space Station, alarm clocks wake astronauts.

Strapped in to keep from floating, a group of astronauts gets some rest aboard the shuttle orbiter Discovery during a 2007 mission.

Where to Sleep

In microgravity, astronauts can sleep just about anywhere—on the floor, the ceiling, or a wall. They can sleep lying down or in an upright position.

To keep from floating in their sleep, astronauts secure themselves. In the space shuttle orbiter, they may sleep in bunks, in sleeping bags, or in chairs with a seatbelt. In the International Space Station, they may use bunks that look like a cross between a school locker and a broom closet. A sleeping bag hangs from a wall of each bunk. STS-119 Mission Specialist Richard Arnold said that the hardest part about sleeping was that he couldn't rest his head on a pillow.

Astronaut Sandra Magnus poses for a photo in her bunk aboard the International Space Station in 2009.

Scientists have found that light in the orbiter and in the International Space Station disrupts astronauts' sleep. Astronauts wear watches that measure and record light and movement data. They keep logs about their sleep patterns. Scientists use the data to improve sleeping conditions in space and to help people on Earth who have trouble getting to sleep.

You Do the Math

Circling Earth

The orbiter circles Earth once every 90 minutes. How many times does the orbiter circle Earth in 24 hours, or one day?

Landing

When the shuttle orbiter returns to Earth, it lands on a runway. Most shuttle landings take place at the Kennedy Space Center in Florida. Shuttles can also land at Edwards Air Force Base in California.

It takes about an hour to get from orbit to the runway. With the orbiter facing backward in orbit, the pilot fires engines to slow down the orbiter. This **deorbit burn** lasts 3 to 4 minutes.

When a shuttle lands, a parachute opens to help slow it down. In this photo, Discovery lands at the end of a 2006 flight.

Into the Atmosphere

The orbiter enters the atmosphere at an angle. Astronauts use computers to make sure that the angle is correct. Too small an angle would cause the orbiter to bounce off the top of the atmosphere. Too steep an angle would cause the orbiter to come down too fast.

The orbiter contacts air in Earth's atmosphere at about 75 to 80 miles above Earth's surface. Astronauts' computers adjust the angle of the orbiter to the airflow. If the orbiter faces into the airflow, the nose and front edges of the wings have too much air **friction**, or force that resists movement. If the orbiter's nose is too high, then its belly has too much friction.

The air gets denser as the orbiter gets lower. The orbiter uses the air to fly like a glider. To slow down, the orbiter banks (tilts) in a series of four turns. The orbiter's path looks like a squiggle.

The pilot takes over manual controls. At last, the orbiter touches the runway at about 220 miles an hour. A parachute opens to slow it down. Home!

You Do the Math

Slowing Down in the Deorbit Burn

During the final orbit, the orbiter travels at 17,322 miles per hour. The deorbit burn slows it by 205 miles per hour. How fast does the orbiter travel right after the deorbit burn?

If You Want to Be an Astronaut

What you need to be a NASA astronaut has changed over the years. The first astronauts were military test pilots. Now, crews include people with a variety of backgrounds. Pilots and commanders still have experience as military pilots and are often test pilots.

Other types of astronauts are Mission Specialists and Payload Specialists. Mission Specialists might be scientists, schoolteachers, engineers, or medical doctors. Payload Specialists work for companies or research organizations. They have detailed knowledge of the payload (cargo) on a particular mission.

Many astronauts studied mathematics, science, or engineering in college. NASA chooses astronaut crews based on the goals of a future mission. Sometimes, crews include astronauts from other countries. Sometimes, U.S. astronauts are members of other countries' crews.

NASA astronaut crews begin training 2 to 3 years before their mission. They practice everything they will do in space while training on Earth.

Answer Key

Pages 4-5: Countdown:
5 minutes 30 seconds. Find the difference between 7 minutes 30 seconds and 2 minutes. Think: 7 minutes 30 seconds minus 2 minutes, or what plus 2 minutes equals 7 minutes 30 seconds?

Pages 6-7: Liftoff:
About 4,200,000 pounds. Round the numbers to the greatest place value. Each solid rocket booster: 1,000,000 pounds; external tank: 2,000,000 pounds; orbiter: 200,000 pounds. Add. 1,000,000 + 1,000,000 + 2,000,000 + 200,000 = 4,200,000.

Pages 8-9: In Earth Orbit:
The temperature range is 400°F. The range is the difference between the greater and lesser numbers. To find the difference, you can count the degrees between ⁻150°F and 250°F on a number line.

Pages 10-11: Rendezvous in Space:
140 miles. Subtract 220 from 360 to find the difference between the altitudes: 360 − 220 = 140.

Pages 12-13: Microgravity:
The astronaut might be 5 feet $10\frac{1}{4}$ inches tall. Add 5 feet $9\frac{1}{2}$ inches and $\frac{3}{4}$ inch. First, add the fractions. Think of $\frac{1}{2}$ as $\frac{2}{4}$, so $\frac{2}{4} + \frac{3}{4} = \frac{5}{4} = 1\frac{1}{4}$. Next, add the feet and inches: 5 feet 9 inches + $1\frac{1}{4}$ inches = 5 feet $10\frac{1}{4}$ inches.

Pages 14-15: The International Space Station:
20.5 tons. To find the total, add. But first, write 32,000 pounds as tons. Think, 32,000 ÷ 2,000 = 16, so 32,000 pounds is 16 tons. Then, 16 + 4.5 = 20.5.

Pages 16-17: Working in Space:
STS-43, STS-105, STS-113, STS-115, STS-120, STS-126. Use place value to order the numbers. 43 has no hundreds, so it goes first. The hundreds are the same in the other numbers. Compare the tens and then the ones.

Pages 18-19: Spacewalk:
The total weight is 786 pounds. To find the total number of pounds, add the three numbers in any order, for example: 315 + 437 + 34 = 786.

Pages 20-21: Foods for Space:
About 210 pounds of food. Multiply the numbers in any order. Here is one way to multiply: 3 x (5 x 14) = 3 x 70 = 210.

Pages 22-23: Exercise and Recreation:
5 miles. Add 5.6, 4.3, 3.7, 4.8, 6.4, 5.0, and 5.2 to find the total number of miles for 7 days. Look for easy-to-add pairs: 5.6 and 6.4, 4.3 and 3.7, 4.8 and 5.2. Don't forget 5.0. To find the average, divide the sum, 35, by 7.

Pages 24-25: Sleep:
The orbiter circles Earth 16 times. To find out how many 90-minute periods are in 24 hours, first write both numbers with the same unit (minutes or hours), and then divide. Remember that there are 60 minutes in an hour and that 90 minutes is the same as 1.5 hours. 24 hours ÷ 1.5 hours = 16, or 1,440 minutes ÷ 90 minutes = 16. You decide which method to solve the problem makes sense to you.

Pages 26-27: Landing:
17,117 miles per hour. To find the slower speed, subtract. 17,322 − 205 = 17,117.

Glossary

average—The sum of a group of numbers divided by the number of addends in the group; also called the mean.

canister—A container, often in the shape of a cylinder.

cosmonaut—A Russian astronaut.

data—Information.

deorbit burn—A blast from rocket engines that slows a spacecraft for reentry into the atmosphere.

external tank—The largest part of the space shuttle system; it contains fuel for the orbiter's three main engines during launch into space.

friction—A force that resists movement and causes heat.

galley—A kitchen on a spacecraft, aircraft, or boat.

microgravity—A barely noticeable amount of gravity that astronauts experience in orbit.

NASA—The National Aeronautics and Space Administration, the government agency that runs the United States' civilian space program.

observatory—A structure with a telescope or other equipment to observe objects in space.

orbit—A circular or elliptical path around a body such as Earth.

orbiter—The part of the space shuttle system that includes the astronauts' cabin and the payload bay. It goes into orbit, returns to Earth and lands like a glider, and then can be used again on future missions.

payload bay—A place on the space shuttle for storing cargo.

polygon—A closed two-dimensional figure that consists of three or more line segments.

satellite—An object that orbits another object. Satellites can be human-made (such as the shuttle orbiter) or natural bodies (such as the Moon, which orbits Earth).

solid rocket booster—One of two rockets that helps propel the space shuttle during launch.

thrust—A force that moves a rocket or spacecraft forward.

thruster—A small engine that the orbiter fires to move in space.

visor—The clear part of a helmet that protects a pilot or astronaut's face.

To Learn More

Read these books:

Aldrin, Buzz. *Reaching for the Moon*. New York: HarperCollins, 2005.

Florian, Douglas. *Comets, Stars, the Moon, and Mars: Space Poems and Painting*. Orlando, Fla.: Harcourt, 2007.

McCarthy, Meghan. *Astronaut Handbook*. New York: Knopf, 2008.

Peterson, Judy Monroe. *Exploring Space: Astronauts & Astronomers*. New York: Rosen Publishing, 2009.

Thimmesh, Catherine. *Team Moon: How 400,000 People Landed Apollo 11 on the Moon*. Boston: Houghton Mifflin, 2006.

Look up these Web sites:

Bill Nye the Science Guy
http://www.billnye.com

Hubble Site
http://www.hubblesite.org

National Aeronautics and Space Administration (NASA), for Students
http://www.nasa.gov/audience/forkids/home/index.html

Key Internet search terms:

astronaut, International Space Station, NASA, space shuttle

Index

About the Author

Mary Hense has always loved planes and spaceships. When she was a girl, she and her brother Jim built model planes. As a Girl Scout, she gave talks about constellations at a planetarium. Now, after developing textbooks for more than 30 years, she enjoys air shows and NASA exhibits. From her backyard in Florida, she can see rockets take off from the Kennedy Space Center, which is more than 60 miles away!